studied Law at Exeter University. She later trained
as a teacher and has taught at all levels from primary
to adult. The author of over 100 children's titles including
the best-selling *Vlad the Drac*, Ann's first book for
Frances Lincoln was *Cinderella and the Hot Air Balloon*.
She is the founder of Barn Owl Books.

was born in South Africa. She studied Graphic Design
at Newham College, Illustration at Chelsea College of Art
and is now working on her M.A. in Illustration at the
University of Brighton. Shelley's work has been exhibited in
London and Brighton. Her other books for Frances Lincoln
include *The Bachelor and the Bean* and *Climbing Rosa*.

For Kays, with hopes for a peaceful life – A.J.
For Steve, Matthew and Tanda – S.F.

About the story

*In the early 8th century AD, the Arabs conquered
southern Spain and transformed Cordoba into a centre of wealth
and learning. They pulled down the church and began
building their great mosque (La Mezquita) with its fountain, Courtyard
of the Orange Trees and forest of columns supporting the roof.
It became the second largest mosque in the Islamic world.
When the Christians re-conquered Cordoba in 1236, they converted
the building for Christian use. Spaniards now look back with
pride at the tolerant rule of the Moors when three religions lived peacefully
side by side. Cordobans do not say, "I went to Mass at the Cathedral",
but "I went to Mass at the Mosque".*

The Most Magnificent Mosque copyright © Frances Lincoln Limited 2004
Text copyright © Ann Jungman 2004
Illustrations copyright © Shelley Fowles 2004
Hand-lettering by Andrew van der Merwe

First published in Great Britain and the USA in 2004 by
Frances Lincoln Children's Books, 4 Torriano Mews
Torriano Avenue, London NW5 2RZ
www.franceslincoln.com

Distributed in the USA by Publishers Group West

First paperback edition published in Great Britain in 2006 and in the USA in 2007.

British Library Cataloguing in Publication Data available on request

ISBN 10: 1-84507-085-2
ISBN 13: 978-1-84507-085-4

Printed in Singapore
1 3 5 7 9 8 6 4 2

The Most Magnificent MOSQUE

Ann Jungman

Illustrated by

Shelley Fowles

F

FRANCES LINCOLN
CHILDREN'S BOOKS

The citizens of Cordoba lived in the most beautiful
city in the world. They were extremely proud
of the Great Mosque, which stood right in the middle
of their city. Not only was the mosque wonderful,
but it was surrounded by glorious gardens full of scented
orange trees, sparkling fountains and flowers of every
colour. The Cordobans used to sit in the garden and think
they were in Paradise itself.

The only problem was three naughty boys:
Rashid, who was a Muslim, Samuel who
was Jewish, and Miguel who was Christian.

They ran in and out of the fountains,
they jumped over the flowerbeds.

They used to hide in the gardens
and throw ripe oranges at anyone they saw.

The gardeners Ibrahim and Yacoub tried to catch
the boys, but the three friends were too fast for them.

One day, the boys were dropping oranges on people
as they came out of the mosque. A particularly rotten
orange dropped at the feet of a man in grand clothes.

"Oh no!" cried Rashid. "It's the Caliph himself.
Run for it!"

The three boys tried to escape, but the Caliph's soldiers grabbed them and brought them before the Caliph.

"Caught at last," smiled Ibrahim the gardener, "and by the Caliph's men!"

Yacoub rubbed his hands together. "They're for it now. They'll get ten lashes at least."

"So, young masters, you would throw oranges
at your Caliph, would you?"

"We didn't know it was you, O Great One,"
whispered Rashid.

"Have you done this before?" asked the Caliph sternly.
All three boys looked miserably at their feet and nodded.

"Every day, Your Magnificence," cried the gardeners.
"These three are the bane of our lives."

"Well," said the Caliph, trying hard not to smile, "I can see you will have to be severely punished. I sentence you to work in these gardens every day for three months…"

So the three boys spent three whole months
planting and weeding and watering and trimming.
Yacoub and Ibrahim worked them until they dropped.

After work, the three hot
and tired friends would wander
through the cool mosque.
"I never saw such a beautiful
building," whispered Miguel. "It is much
more magnificent than our church."
"Or my synagogue," sighed Samuel.
"Wondrous and fair indeed."
"Truly our mosque is a house of God," said Rashid.

As the three friends grew up, they saw less and less of each other.

Samuel travelled far and wide trading in spices and silk. He kept a diary

Miguel inherited his father's farm. He became a great land-owner

Rashid studied medicine and became a famous doctor.

telling of his travels and wrote poetry of great beauty.

and was known for his kindness and the lively songs he sang.

The Caliph grew old and enemies began to attack Cordoba from every side. In the end, he was defeated in a great battle by the Christian king Fernando.

Miguel, who was now the most important man in Cordoba,
went to greet his new king.

"Don Miguel," cried the king, "take me to the Great Mosque,
of which I have heard so much."

"With pleasure, Sire," said Miguel. "It is the pride
and joy of all citizens of Cordoba – Muslim,
Christian and Jew alike."

The king looked at the mosque.

"It is indeed a most magnificent mosque," said the king, and he sighed. "But this is to be a Christian city and we shall build a great cathedral on this site. The mosque must be pulled down."

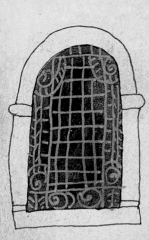

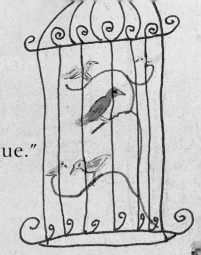

That night, Miguel invited Samuel and Rashid
to dinner.

"My dear old friends, I have terrible news.
The king plans to pull down our beloved mosque."

"What about our wonderful gardens?"
asked Samuel and Rashid.

"They too will go."

"What can we do?" cried Rashid, burying his head in his hands.

"We three must go to the king," said Samuel, "and tell him how precious the mosque is to everyone in Cordoba."

The next day, the people of Cordoba packed into the town square to see the king.

"I am here to plead for our mosque on behalf of all the Christians of Cordoba," cried Miguel.

Everyone cheered.

"I am here on behalf of the Jews of Cordoba," said Samuel.

"Quite right!" shouted the crowd.

"And Sire, I speak for the Muslim citizens. Spare our mosque!" cried Rashid.

Everyone cheered even louder.

"Well, well," said the king. "Three communities with one voice. I can see that I will have no friends here if I pull down your mosque."

He thought for a moment. Then he said, "I will build a church in a small part of the mosque, but the rest of the building and the gardens shall belong to all you good people of Cordoba."

Cheers echoed throughout the square.

So the Great Mosque was left for future generations to enjoy and wonder at. It is still there today, and millions of people visit it every year. Many sit in the gardens and enjoy the shady trees and sweet-scented blossom – and a few visitors say they have even seen the ghosts of three naughty boys running in and out of the fountains.